The Patient

Robert A. Valentine

PAGE PUBLISHING
Conneaut Lake, PA

First originally published by Page Publishing 2022

ISBN 978-1-6624-8730-9 (pbk)
ISBN 978-1-6624-8731-6 (digital)

Printed in the United States of America

CHAPTER 1

"This is Dr. Caitlyn Wells for Patient Evaluation. The patient is Dr. Corey Laenz and is known to have killed over a hundred of his patients."

"All right, let's begin. So, Corey, how are you feeling today?"

"Please call me Dr. Laenz, I insist."

"No, please answer the question."

"You're being a bit rude, Doc. You know what I should do instead?"

"What?"

"This."

"Corey, put the scalpel down now. Orderlies!"

"They're not going to get here in time, darling."
End of audio.

CHAPTER 2

"This is Dr. Abigale Rose for patient reevaluation. The patient is Dr. Corey Laenz."

"So, Dr. Laenz, how did you manage to sneak a scalpel past security?"

"I can't tell you that."

"Why not, Dr. Laenz?"

"That's patient-doctor confidentiality. Are these restraints really necessary?"

"Why do say that? Dr. Caitlyn was so disfigured by what you did that she committed suicide in the hospital. So yes, the restraints are necessary."

"She killed herself, huh. I find that funny. Hahaha, what a killing joke that is, hahaha! The irony in all that."

"Dr. Laenz, do you take pleasure in those that you killed?"

"Pleasure…hmm…never thought of it like that. Let's put it in terms on my level. You ever did an autopsy on a corpse? It's not in the least remotely fascinating. Cutting a live person open—now that's a different story. The screams of agony is simply a symphony to my ears."

"Do you hear voices, Dr. Laenz?"

"No…wait, no. Why do you ask?"

"It's just a procedure. The next question is, are you afraid of what you've become over the years?"

"That is the wrong question to ask. It's not what I have become over the years. It's what I have been over the years."

"Care to elaborate, Dr. Laenz?"

"Gladly. Let's start with my childhood."

CHAPTER 3

"**M**y childhood was not normal. You see, my mom was a raging alcoholic, and my dad…let's just say he had demons that completely possessed him. If he wasn't beating me within an inch of my life, he was out drinking. You know, late binges that made him smell like he soaked in a brewery vat. Even after all these years, I can still smell the alcohol. I started thinking what made a person, so I don't know mad all the time.

"One night, I was maybe sixteen or seventeen, I drugged both my parents. My mother died like I intended. She wasn't part of this monster's dissection. I tied my dad to the dining room table, and I waited for him to awake from his stupor. I remember his face. First, it was bewilderment, followed by rage, then he noticed I held a kitchen knife in my hand."

"Hold on, Dr. Laenz. You said your mother died the way you intended. What did you mean by that?"

"I mixed morphine, heroine, and a liquefied form of Thorazine in her drink, gin being her go to drink."

"You mean to tell me you gave your own mother a Brompton cocktail?"

"In less words, yes."

"Do you regret it?"

"No, why would I?"

"No remorse, no feeling, nothing?"

"Why would I do something so meaningless if I didn't gain something from it?"

"What did you gain from it?"

"Complete and total satisfaction, knowing that I single handedly freed my own mother from a marriage she was eternally damned too."

"Please go on about your father."

CHAPTER 4

"Ahh, the first time I cut into a living being was absolutely satisfying. The endorphins gave me a mental high so exuberating I'll never forget it. The screams were mental ecstasy. I loved every second of it. I cut his chest open, watching the crimson river of life, flowing profusely. Come to think of it, I painted the dining room walls with his blood. His screams alone were enough to wake the neighbors, so the last thing I wanted to see him do is see him drown in the thing that's been plaguing him."

"Alcohol?"

"Precisely. How I did it was absolutely wonderful. You see, he completely passed out from the pain. So I stitched him back up and stuck him in a thirty-gallon tub full of ice. You see, by this time, he lost a large quantity of blood, so I gave him a blood transfusion. My father was once a renowned surgeon in his day. He had a home-based surgical room for, you know, under the table emergency surgery.

"When he awoke from the blood loss, he managed to get enough sense to know he was a dead man. I plugged his nose with enough gauze to choke him, but fortunately, he was still breathing through his mouth. I got a tube and shoved it deep down his throat and watched the best delight in years, watching that insolent little maggot, struggling against his own poison. And finally choking on alcohol, blood, and vomit. For years I suffered in which no child should, and I loved every minute of his suffering."

"I think that's enough for today, Dr. Laenz."

"Do you not want to hear more, Dr. Rose? Hmm…maybe I should tell what I did to my own mother after I killed her."

"Orderlies, please get Dr. Laenz out of my sight now."

The orderlies carted Dr. Laenz off as he yelled, "I embalmed her, Dr. Rose. I embalmed her. Hahaha." His maniacal laugh echoed off the stone corridor. Abigale knew she was going to have nightmares after today.

CHAPTER 5

"Do you sleep well knowing what horrors await you today, Dr. Rose?"

"You don't scare me, Dr. Laenz. I made a complete psychological profile of you last night, and I slept well. Thank you very much."

"Do I sense cockiness, or are you that self-satisfied of your pride? Just remember, monsters are born, not made."

"I disagree with you, Dr. Laenz. You see, I took note of the fact you suffer from severe delusions, paranoia, low self-esteem, narcissism, sanguineous, manic episodes, and a complete disregard for human life. Am I wrong, Dr. Laenz?"

"Well, you've already lied to me, Dr. Rose."

"And how did I do that, Dr. Laenz?"

"I've noticed the heavily made-up eyes. The eye shadow does not conjoin with the severe puffiness around your eyes, common in those people who have insomnia or just witnessed talking to a living monster with, what did you say, a complete disregard for human life?"

Dr. Rose felt like Dr. Laenz just pried open her head and poured a five-pound bag of ice in her skull.

"Just simple observations, Dr. Rose."

"I looked over your police report, Dr. Laenz, and it doesn't say when or even the fact that you caused your parents death."

"Really? I suppose the fact got expunged from my record. I so badly wanted to become a renowned surgeon like my own father."

"That's another thing, Dr. Laenz. I didn't come across your father's history as a surgeon."

"Didn't I tell you it was under the table? Hmm… under the table. That's quite hilarious. Hahaha."

"Even as you say, Dr. Laenz, there still would be hospital follow-ups to make sure the surgery was a success—paper trails, something that would lead back to your father."

"Not a chance. You see, the patients always paid upfront with cash, and the follow-ups were no problem because my father was perfect until the poisonous swill that he drank clouded his mind until he became slave to it."

CHAPTER 6

"**A**lso, the police report has a bit of a mistake."

"How's that, Dr. Rose?"

"The report says you killed over a hundred of your patients, but only 90 percent of your patients have been found. Care to elaborate?"

"Certainly. Have you ever thought of the fact that I might've pieced together my own friends, kind of something out of Mary Shelley, isn't it?"

"Are you saying you've made things out of your victims like freaking mannequins?"

"I can't say exactly."

"Why not?"

"I promised them I would never break doctor-patient confidentiality. Hahaha."

That laugh will forever haunt my nightmares, Abigael thought to herself.

"Let's just say they like to talk to me."

"Are you saying that the dead talk to you?"

"In a manner of speaking, they don't speak the way you and I carry on a conversation. But in their own way. You see, the dead have their own language, and I'm the only one that can converse with them. Hahaha."

Abigale cursed herself for doing a psycho analysis on this raving lunatic. "Need I remind you, Corey, that I am supposed to see if you're sane enough to stand trial?" Her icy blue eyes pierced through his stone-gray ones, hoping to find a weakness, perhaps vulnerability. There was nothing but dead, emotionless, gray eyes staring back almost piercing through her skull.

"Now listen here, Abigale." She flinched. Him knowing her first name was strictly forbidden. "I will eventually give names of my, well, let's say, my saved individuals on account of a few bargains."

Abigale exploded, "You don't get to make bargains here, Corey! I'm here to analyze and get rid of you forever! Orderlies!"

As the orderlies went to cart off the mad doctor, he, in a cool, collective, tone, which really unnerved Abigale, simply said, "Washington Drive 574, Lot 23."

CHAPTER 7

"**G**ood, God Almighty," Abigale said under her breath.

Looking at the photographs taken from the warehouse, the storage space was a fucking nightmare. Abigale already vomited three times in her home bowl. Perhaps more was to come. The storage walls were covered in some type of padding, probably to soundproof the interior. On various meat hooks hanging from the rafters were unidentifiable masses of flesh. The walls were colored in what Abigale thought was maroon paint but was actually years of dried blood. The tile floor was spotless. From reading the police report, there was a drain in the center of the floor, connecting to a larger draining system. And finally, a mummified woman on a steel autopsy table. The coroners actually had to scrape the body off the tabletop.

A faded toe tag read, "Allison Marie Laenz."

That fucking monster was telling the truth. He literally embalmed his own mother, she thought to herself. Abigale felt a metallic, copper taste in her mouth and made a mad dash to her bathroom, barely making it before she vomited the rest of the contents in her stomach.

CHAPTER 8

"**S**o did you like my little present, Dr. Rose? I figure I let bygones be bygones, considering you insulted me first." Corey was in the dolly that transports him in and out of sessions, surrounded by a massive orderly to maintain Corey's actions.

"Dr. Laenz, if you please be so kind as to enlighten me on the contents of the warehouse."

"First, I want a few things out of you. Tit for tat."

"I'll have to talk to Supervisor Green for any kind of deal or bargain."

"So should I take that as a no?" His smile showed his missing right top lateral incisor apparently from a victim who tried to fight back, but to no avail. It was the smile of an apex predator.

"I didn't exactly say no, but I can't say yes."

"Here, think about it, dear Miss Rose. Franklin, my dear boy, reach inside my breast pocket and hand my psychiatrist the contents." Franklin hesitated, perhaps considering the fact his fingers would be inches from this nutcase's mouth. Franklin put a massive hand on Corey's throat, thrusting backward and finally reached inside and pulled out a small slip of paper.

"Here, Dr. Rose." Franklin handed the note to Abigale. She quickly read it and put it in her jeans pocket.

"Now the contents of the warehouse, Dr. Laenz."

"My thoughts exactly, Dr. Rose."

CHAPTER 9

"From what I can infer, you've seen poor, dear Mother on the table. Mummified, void of all life, yes?"

Abigale nodded. Corey smiled once more at her, that same predator-eats-prey grin.

"She was the first of many to be saved."

"If I may ask what was or who was hanging from the meat hooks?"

"Oh, those filthy little things? Nothing more than pieces of garbage. Herman Silas, for one. You know who that is, right?"

"Unfortunately. The owner of the warehouse lot, right?"

"Exactly, what's today?"

"The twenty-third of March, Dr. Laenz."

"You do the math, sweetheart, and I'll continue. Most of the bodies are nothing more than insignificant little specks of human waste. Winos and such.

Perhaps you'll be surprised by a bigger name or two. Reverend Smith, who tried to convert me on something supposably big, all bullshit though. And finally, LeAnn and Carter Rose, both renowned humanitarians, who left a hefty fortune to some girl." He smiled once more looking right at Abigale and finished, "Perhaps I'm looking right at that girl."

"Franklin, take him away." As Franklin carted off Corey, Abigale heard the lunatic's laugh echo off the stony corridor's long hallway.

CHAPTER 10

Abigale looked at a thick manila envelope on her kitchen table. The same package had been sitting there a week before Corey's admittance into LaCroix Asylum. Abigale remembered the postman, saying it was a special delivery paid by a Mr. Dorian Black. Abigale sat down, hesitated, then tore the package open, the contents falling out.

"Son of a bitch," Abigale muttered to herself.

It was the pictures of both her parents in various positions. Her father was shaven bald with nails stuck in various places in and around his head almost like a crown, shattered wrists, and sliced Achilles' tendons. Her mother, on the other hand, had her eyes and groin stitched shut and her finger and toenails removed as well as each of their tongues removed. With surgical extractions, several organs were removed as well. A small note stuck to the back of the picture of her father. Abigale read and reread the note half a dozen times, perhaps looking for some error, but it was to no avail. She cried into the long hours of the night. She fell asleep, dreaming of her parents.

CHAPTER 11

"**M**r. Green, may ask about your opinions on Corey's request?" Abigale asked politely.

Walter Green was the head supervisor in the psychological department of LaCroix Asylum, perhaps as a better term, the warden.

"Hmm…did you read this before giving it to me, Miss Rose?"

"Yes, sir. Yesterday, as a matter of fact, during our last session. He had Franklin give me the requests in order to strike a bargain." Abigale squirmed a little in her seat. Being in Walter's presence was enough to unnerve any one, including the more dangerous patients.

Abigale once heard Walter was in the army as a trained sniper and got an honorable discharge within a ten-year stint.

"I, Dr. Corey Aleister Laenz, as my first request, would like to gaze under the stars once more before my sentencing begins and ends." Walter adjusted his bifocals and asked, "You know what this sounds like, Miss Rose?"

"No, sir."

"It sounds like a load of horse shit." Walter cleared his throat and continued, "My second request is simple. I would like a dinner made up of a rare steak, mashed potatoes with a side of vegetables served with a glass of Cabernet Sauvignon. This guy is a goddamn fruitcake."

"Corey has promised me more information on his victims, including those that are still missing, Mr. Green."

"Hmm…perhaps we should enlighten the doctor. Actually, let's wait until tomorrow to further discuss the situation." Abigale went to say something, perhaps to argue, but Walter raised a hand to stop her and said, "Dismissed."

Abigale nodded and left Walter's office.

CHAPTER 12

"So what did Supervisor Green say, my dear?" Corey said with that cold smile.

"He said to wait until tomorrow, if you must know, Dr. Laenz." A dark cloud rode across Corey's face. Abigale's interpretation of that cloud told her Corey was about to pounce.

He can't do anything. He's restrained as well as guarded by Franklin's mastodon-like body, she reassured herself. The storm passed, and Corey's face went into that dead expression once.

"I believe our session is up, my dear Abigale."

A cold chill passed through her spine. "How do you know my name, Dr. Laenz?"

"Oh, another question for another time perhaps." Another maniacal laughter exploded from him. She nodded at Franklin to take him away.

CHAPTER 13

Walter Green was always the last to leave the psych ward, filling out paperwork and time-stamping sessions, as well splitting up the payroll per orderly. It was exhausting, but it took off the pain off his wife's recent passing.

Footsteps echoed through the corridor. Walter's faded hearing didn't register the footfalls until a banging on his office door startled him. Knowing it might be an orderly picking up his paycheck, he reached for the doorknob when his combat senses went off. He quietly walked away from the door. The banging continued and then stopped suddenly. Walter reached in the bottom drawer behind his desk, hoping to get the drop on the attacker. A chair came flying through the office's glass window, barely missing Walter. A hand from the other side opened the door, a figure strode in with a steak knife, making headway toward Walter in a fast, fluent motions. The stranger stabbed Walter over twenty-five times before the gun was freed. His bloody hand dropped the gun back in the drawer, knowing his life was forfeit. The stranger left the office with Walter's keys to the outside.

CHAPTER 14

Abigale's phone began ringing as she was in the middle of drying her hair from getting out of the shower. She picked it up. "Hello?" Nothing at first, so she repeated herself, saying, "Hello?"

A choked voice said, "He's free."

Abigale registered two things in a matter of seconds: one, that was Walter's voice in a very faint way, which was unlike him; and two, if what he said is true, her life is in danger.

Abigale got dressed as quickly as possible, then rang for the police. "Hello, operator, I'd like to report a murder at LaCroix Asylum, and I think the killer is coming after me."

A voice on the other end said, "We'll send a patrol out at once. Please stay where you're at. We have an officer coming to your location immediately."

Abigale hung up the phone. As she did, the power went out in her apartment building. She couldn't see anything except her front door. She cautiously opened the door and peered out. The whole apartment hallway was dark. She cautiously took a few steps forward, wondering why people weren't coming out, then remembering this particular floor had faulty wiring, causing power outages often. As she turned back to go back into her apartment, a heavy instrument cracked her across the back of the skull. As she faded into oblivion, she looked up into the doctor's face.

CHAPTER 15

Milwaukee Gazette
March 25, 2000

Police have started a massive manhunt in search of the mass murderer, Dr. Corey Theodore Laenz. It has been stated that he's kidnapped Dr. Abigale Melissa Rose, an up-and-coming psychiatrist. Furthermore, he has, in his escape from LaCroix Asylum, murdered at least sixteen people, including head supervisor, Walter Green. No one has figured out how he managed to escape, considering all cells are locked tight with keycard access only.

CHAPTER 16

Milwaukee Gazette Article 2
April 1, 2000

Police have still not found any trace of either Corey Laenz nor his victim, Abigale Rose. Police have had several anonymous tips come in, but all have been proven useless. Some evidence has come to light that Abigale is a surviving victim and orphan heir to the Rose family fortune because of Corey Laenz's previous murder spree. People are speculating that he has always been targeting Miss. Rose since her survival on the attack of her family.

CHAPTER 17

Milwaukee Gazette Article 3
April 8, 2000

Police have received a letter in the form of the doctor's handwriting. It describes that he doesn't have Abigale, but his longtime assistant, Dorian Black, has done a live autopsy on her, and her organs will be sent to the police in alphabetical order. Perhaps this is a ploy set up by the unpredictable doctor. If so, may Abigale rest in peace alongside her parents, LeAnn and Carter Rose. Their fortune will be frozen in their account until the next of kin comes and claims it, or Abigale is proven to be alive.

CHAPTER 18

Milwaukee Gazette Article 4
April 15, 2000

Police have called off the search for Dr. Corey Theodore Laenz and his victim, Dr. Abigale Melissa Rose. They are calling the case cold until further notice, but perhaps is more intriguing is the assistant, Dorian Black, is believed to be nothing more than a psychotic personality of Corey Laenz. Despite that fact, people, including police, have declared Abigale Melissa Rose deceased.

CHAPTER 19

Abigale stirred from her morphine-induced state, "Ah good morning, darling, hope you slept well."

Corey's laugh rang through what seemed to be a modified storm shelter. Abigale went to speak when she felt a smooth cylindrical object in her mouth. She spat it out. A hand reached and smacked her hard across the face.

Corey's eyes glowed angrily at her. "You do that again, Miss Rose, and I'll personally pull out all your teeth myself with rusty pliers. That tube is to help you breathe. Your tongue has been freshly harvested. So in order for you not to choke on the blood, I gave you the tube." He jammed it back into her mouth. He turned his back to her and walked out of her sight, humming as he went.

Judging by the ravings of the doctor, she had been abducted and experimented on for the past few weeks. Even more than that, she knew she'd been pumped full of a pharmacy drugs through an IV drip in her arm. She shivered as a cool breeze drafted through the cellar. He took her clothes off as soon they got to this abandoned farmhouse just on the outskirts of Milwaukee, a rural no-name town that's been long since abandoned.

"I'm almost done harvesting your organs. Well, the ones I want anyway." He winked and laughed his maniacal laugh. He pulled apart an already started wound. "Now you see this little IV bag." He pointed to a small pouch containing a murky liquid. "This is placines, a potent drug to keep your blood pressure going at a steady rate. I wouldn't want you to miss all the fun, dear."

He started his operations well into the morning hours, yawning. He put his tools aside and stitched up Abigale and sincerely said, "Now don't go any-where. I'll be back after a little bit of sleep, unlike you." He laughed at his own joke as he left the cellar.

Abigale stirred once more from her semicon-scious state. Her left wrist, despite being a bit man-gled, had slipped free from the table cuff. She spat the tube out from her mouth again, noticing the miracle of her hand being free. Trying to shake off the morphine, she struggled for what seemed to be hours, but it could've been just mere minutes to take off the right cuff before it finally came free.

She struggled to her feet, wincing at the stiffness coming from all parts of her body. She looked around at her surroundings when a noise above her head shook her once more from the drug induced stupor.

He's coming back, Abigael thought, *I have to hide.*

She tried to run, but her legs gave out. Corey's voice rang out, "Dear little Abby, it's been a few hours since our last visit. Are you decent?" He chuckled at his little sadistic joke. Abigale heard keys jingling, knowing she had a matter of seconds to hide. She made a dash toward a cabinet when she tripped over something large and heavy. It took her a second to grab it. The cellar door opened. His eyes adjusted to the descending sun, realizing the operating table was empty. A moment too late when he came down the cellar steps and saw a cinder block come crashing down on his head. The impact made a sickening splat. Gray matter painted the cellar walls with each repetitive blow. Abigale, bleeding from her torn stitches, dashed outside with an overwhelming and dizzying feeling of freedom.

CHAPTER 20

William Rogers, a big country boy, went on his way to Peck's Roadhouse. He was a bouncer there, the ruffians always went to Peck's to start a fight when a naked woman came darting out in front of his truck.

"Jesus Christ." He slammed on his brakes, did a one eighty, and stopped. The woman came running up to him. She was covered in blood and in what seemed a blind panic. "What's the matter with ya? Ya crazy or something?"

The woman shook her head, then her eyes frosted over and passed out. William caught her in his massive arms. He carried her to his truck and gently put her in.

"All righty, miss. I'm gonna take ya to the hospital. You'll be right as rain." He didn't know if she heard or not, but it made him feel better.

EPILOGUE

Milwaukee Gazette Article 5

Miss Abigale Melissa Rose has been found alive by a bouncer named William Rogers, who's been hailed as a hero. Miss Rose, despite the previous injuries inflicted on her, directed the police to a farmhouse where she was held captive. Officers did find an unrecognizable mass in the cellar. Dental records showed that it was Miss Rose's captor, Dr. Corey Theodore Laenz. Miss Rose has decided on shying away from the public despite surviving a second time from Dr. Laenz's assault.

She has been seen around town on occasion with William Rogers. Perhaps a love affair has spawned between the two of them. William Rogers has declined any and all interviews for the both of them. That being said, off the record, he has said he and Abigale have mutually agreed on moving to his hometown in Nebraska to avoid any more troubles. So as their time comes to move on and leave Milwaukee and head for Nebraska, the fortune of their lives enhances as time marches on.

ABOUT THE AUTHOR

Robert A. Valentine resides in Arkansas with his loving family. In his spare time, he writes about personal experiences.